THE

# ASIAN KETO & LOW-CARB

## COOKBOOK

**SISTERS SOM ALLISON & TIPPY WYATT**

# Dedication

To my parents who have taught and given me the inspiration for the love of cooking.

My husband and daughter, thank you for your ongoing support and love through this wonderful process and every aspect of life!

Last but not least, my wonder family who have supported us throughout this process. Truly grateful for everyone!

With xoxo,

*Som Allison*

To my husband Ryan, my lifelong partner, my lifelong inspiration.

To my family, my root to all flowers.

To you, thank you.

With Love + Gratitude,

*Tippy Wyatt*

---

## "WHEN YOU COOK WITH PASSION AND LOVE, YOU COOK AUTHENTICALLY."

### TIPPY WYATT + SOM ALLISON

---

 YouTube TippyTales           @tippywyatt          www.TippyTales.com

# CONTENTS

## SOUPS

| | |
|---|---|
| Lao Boat | 39 |
| Mixed Veggie Red Curry | 42 |
| Lao Egg Soup | 44 |
| Tom Kha | 46 |
| Om Gai | 47 |
| Kimchi Jjigae | 50 |

## SALADS

| | |
|---|---|
| Cucumber Salad | 54 |
| Asian Chopped Chicken Salad | 55 |
| Yum Salad | 57 |
| Papaya Salad | 60 |
| Cucumber Kimchi Salad | 62 |

## SIDES

| | |
|---|---|
| Teppanyaki Zoodles | 66 |
| Garlic Chinese Broccoli | 68 |
| Water Spinach Sauté | 70 |
| Blistered Shishito Peppers | 72 |
| Bok Choy | 74 |
| Sautéed Long Beans | 76 |

## SAUCES

| | |
|---|---|
| Chili Oil | 80 |
| Spicy Mayo | 82 |
| Mushroom Jeow | 84 |
| Tomato Jeow | 86 |
| Spicy Lemongrass Jeow | 88 |
| Jeow Som | 90 |

# RECOMMENDED

## PRODUCTS/SAUCES

———————

Here are the recommended brands of Asian sauces we use throughout the cookbook. You can use which ever you can get access to but these are preferred due to the authentic taste.

———————————————————

**THREE CRAB
FISH SAUCE**

**RED BOAT
FISH SAUCE**

(No sugar)

**LEE KUM KEE
GLUTEN FREE
OYSTER SAUCE**

**BRAGG'S LIQUID
AMINOS**

**SAIGON BADEK**

(Fermented Fish Sauce)

# ENTREES

# SHRIMP BUTTER LETTUCE WRAPS

Whenever our mother would tell us she was going to make shrimp wraps, all of us kids would make it a priority to get their shrimp wrap cravings satisfied. Yes, it is that good. The freshness of the lettuce and herbs along with the crunchiness of the vegetables topped with the blanched shrimps, drizzled with the lemongrass herb jeow is just undeniably one of the best recipes to us in this whole entire cookbook. Now do yourself a favor and stop drooling and start making this!

✱Pair this with our Spicy Lemongrass Jeow (pg. 88)

| PREP TIME | COOK TIME | SKILL LEVEL | RECIPE |
|---|---|---|---|
| 15 MINUTES | 3 MINUTES | EASY | LOW-CARB |

**SERVINGS: 4    CALORIES: 137    FATS: 2G    PROTEIN: 23G    CARBS: 2G**

## INGREDIENTS

10 cups water

1 lb. shrimp

2 heads of butter lettuce

Sliced cucumber

Thinly sliced carrot sticks

Cilantro

## STEPS

1. Bring water to a boil in large pot

2. Blanch the shrimp in boiling water for about 3 mins and then set aside

3. Arrange 1-2 butter lettuce leaves on plate then top with 3-4 shrimp, sliced cucumber, carrot sticks, and cilantro

4. Serve with lemongrass jeow dipping sauce **See lemongrass jeow dipping sauce recipe pg. 88

# PORK HERB PATTY

You won't find this anywhere else! It's our mother's homemade original recipe and we are so proud and thrilled to share it with you now! Those that have had the privilege to try it say it reminds them of meatloaf that has been enhanced with incredible aromatic herbs. Unlike meatloaf, it isn't baked. Instead, these wonderful little meat patties are fried in avocado oil to perfection. This recipe will always hold a special place in our cookbook and our hearts. Enjoy!

**PREP TIME**
30 MINUTES

**COOK TIME**
15-20 MINUTES

**SKILL LEVEL**
INTERMEDIATE

**RECIPE**
KETO

**SERVINGS: 4     CALORIES: 503     FATS: 37G     PROTEIN: 30G     CARBS: 6G**

## INGREDIENTS

1 medium shallot

5 gloves of garlic

3-6 Thai chilies

4 kaffir lime leaves (sliced)

2-3 cups avocado oil

⅓ cup cilantro

1 ½ lb. ground pork

2 tbsps gluten-free oyster sauce

1 tbsp fish sauce

Pinch of salt

1 egg

## STEPS

1.  In a food processor add in garlic, shallots, Thai chilies, kaffir lime leaves (sliced), cilantro and blend until fine

2.  In a separate bowl, add in ground pork, oyster sauce, fish sauce, and mixture from step 1

3.  Thoroughly mix all ingredients by hand

4.  Form pork mixture into palm size patties

5.  Add 1 inch of oil to cast iron or nonstick pan and let it heat for 5 minutes on medium heat

6.  Add in palm size patties and cook each side for approx. 3-4 minutes

7.  Let the patties cool on a wire strainer to drain excess oil, then enjoy

# RIBEYE LAAB (SPICY BEEF SALAD)

There are so many ways to make this classic Laotian dish and every restaurant will make their own version. We've tried dozens of variations and now we're sharing how we enjoy it best. The flavorful grilled slices of ribeye mixed with the freshness of herbs and spices is sure to make your mouth water for more.

**PREP TIME**
20 MINUTES

**COOK TIME**
10 MINUTES

**SKILL LEVEL**
INTERMEDIATE

**RECIPE**
KETO

**SERVINGS: 2    CALORIES: 731    FATS: 57G    PROTEIN: 41G    CARBS: 7G**

## INGREDIENTS

1lb. ribeye steak

1 tbsp olive oil

¼ tsp salt

⅛ tsp pepper

½ tsp of liquid aminos

1 tsp avocado oil

1 lime juiced

1 tsp of ground chili flakes

2 ½ tsp of fish sauce

⅓ cup of sliced red onion

⅓ cup of mint

3 tbsps of green onions

3 tbsps of cilantro

3 diced Thai chilies


Optional:

1 English cucumber

8 oz. long beans

## STEPS

1. Marinate ribeye in salt, pepper, liquid amino, and olive oil in fridge for about 30 minutes

2. While steak is marinating, wash then slice red onion, mint, cilantro, green onions, and Thai chilies

3. Heat cast iron on medium heat with 1 tsp of avocado oil

4. Sear steak on all 4 sides for approx. 2 ½ minutes each side

5. Remove steak and let steak rest for 10 minutes, then cut into ¼ inch slices

6. Meanwhile, in a medium bowl add juice of 1 lime, fish sauce, and Thai chilies

7. Combine steak with sauce

8. Add in red onions, green onions, cilantro, and mint - mix and serve

9. Adjust salad to your liking with salt as desired

10. Optional: Serve alongside cucumber and long beans for a refreshing salad

# EGG ROLL IN A BOWL

We couldn't do an Asian cookbook without including egg rolls which are universally known to be a staple in Asian cuisine. This recipe is full of flavor and crunchy veggies to satisfy any egg roll lover. We love to douse this with sriracha sauce or our homemade chili oil (see recipe) to give it that added kick.

| PREP TIME | COOK TIME | SKILL LEVEL | RECIPE |
|---|---|---|---|
| 15 MINUTES | 15 MINUTES | EASY | KETO |

**SERVINGS: 4    CALORIES: 390    FATS: 31G    PROTEIN: 20G    CARBS: 6G**

## INGREDIENTS

2 tbsp avocado oil

2 tbsp garlic minced

1 lb. of ground meat (ground pork, ground beef, ground chicken, or turkey)

1 cup red cabbage (shredded)

1 cup green cabbage (shredded)

1/3 cup carrots (cut into match sticks)

1/2 of a white onion (sliced)

¼ cup of green onions (sliced)

1 tsp of sesame seeds

1 tbsp of Lee Kum Kee oyster sauce

1 tsp of Three Crab fish sauce

1 ½ tsp soy sauce or Bragg's liquid aminos

Salt & pepper to taste

## STEPS

1. Add avocado oil to nonstick pan over medium heat

2. Let oil heat up for one minute then add in minced garlic

3. Sauté garlic for 30 seconds

4. Add in pork, a pinch of salt and pepper

5. Immediately add oyster sauce, fish sauce, liquid aminos

6. Sauté until pork is no longer pink and fully cooked

7. Then add all the vegetables (red & green cabbage, carrots, white onions) except green onions

8. Fold in vegetables to pork mixture until cooked to your liking. (Approx. 2-3 minutes for al dente)

9. Then add in green onions and fold for one minute

10. Turn off heat and sprinkle with sesame seeds

11. Adjust with salt and pepper as desired and serve

10

# BBQ PORK ON A STICK (MOO-PING)

Everyone loves this recipe and when you make it, you'll understand why. It is very hard to not like. The cut of pork is fattier for the juicier bite with this outstanding marinade. We suggest you marinade it 24 hours for the best flavor. A crowd-pleaser and taste bud favorite, without a doubt!

**PREP TIME**
30 MINUTES +
2-24 HOURS OF
MARINATING

**COOK TIME**
15 MINUTES

**SKILL LEVEL**
EASY

**RECIPE**
KETO

**SERVINGS: 4    CALORIES: 433    FATS: 30G    PROTEIN: 30G    CARBS: 7G**

## INGREDIENTS

1 ½ lbs. of pork butt

10 garlic cloves

1 oz lemongrass

3 tbsps of oyster sauce

1 tbsp of fish sauce


Equipment:

Bamboo or metal skewers

Grill

## STEPS

1. Slice pork but into one inch squares that are 1/2 inch thick and add to a large bowl

2. Mince garlic and lemongrass in food processor

3. Add garlic and lemongrass mixture to pork and add in oyster sauce and fish sauce

4. Thoroughly combine all ingredients and let everything marinade for at least 2-24 hours (the longer it marinades the better it will taste)

5. Skewer the pork pieces on to a bamboo or metal skewer

6. Cook pork on bbq grill for 12 to 15 minutes, turning every 2 minutes until the pork reaches an internal temperature of 140 degrees F.

# FRIED CHICKEN WINGS

Mom makes the best chicken wings which are always requested by family and friends for all special gatherings. We knew we needed something similar but on the keto/low carb side. Savory, salty, garlicky, and crispy perfection all in one bite!

✳Pairs with Tomato Jeow (pg. 86)

| PREP TIME | COOK TIME | SKILL LEVEL | RECIPE |
|---|---|---|---|
| 15 MINUTES+ 1 HOUR OF MARINATING | 10 MINUTES | EASY | KETO |

**SERVINGS: 3    CALORIES: 643    FATS: 57G    PROTEIN: 28G    CARBS: 4G**

## INGREDIENTS

2 cups of avocado oil

2 lbs. of chicken wings/drumsticks

2 tbsp of garlic powder

2 tbsp liquid aminos

½ tsp of white pepper

¼ tsp of salt

## STEPS

1. Place chicken in a gallon bag with garlic powder, liquid aminos, white pepper, and salt and let marinade sit for an hour an half in the refrigerator

2. In a pan add 2 cups avocado oil to pan and turn to medium heat **temp should be about 350-375 F

3. Get a plate and cover it with a paper towel and place it by the stove

4. Gently place chicken in oil

5. Cook chicken for approx. 5 minutes. Stir occasionally to make sure all sides of chicken will cook

6. Remove from oil and place onto plate covered with a napkin or paper towel and enjoy!

# TEMPURA COCONUT SHRIMP

A guaranteed crowd pleaser! If you make this, be sure to set aside a couple for yourselves as this will go fast! We love the crunchy texture and coconut taste dipped in a creamy spicy mayo. If you prefer a more citrus twist to your seafood, squeeze a lemon wedge on your shrimp and enjoy!

✱Pairs with Spicy Mayo (pg. 82)

**PREP TIME**
30 MINUTES

**COOK TIME**
5-10 MINUTES

**SKILL LEVEL**
EASY

**RECIPE**
LOW-CARB

**SERVINGS: 3     CALORIES: 329     FATS: 20G     PROTEIN: 8G     CARBS: 11G**

## INGREDIENTS

1 cup coconut flour (½ cup split)

1 egg

1 lb. of peeled shrimp (leave the tail on)

2 cups of avocado oil

Dry Ingredients:

½ cup coconut flour

1 tsp paprika

1 tsp garlic powder

½ tsp salt

½ tsp pepper

¼ tsp ancho chili powder

¼ tsp of salt

Sauce:

½ cup of mayonnaise

1 tsp of Sriracha

¼ tsp of sesame oil

## STEPS

1. Rinse and pat dry 1 lb. of shrimp and place into a paper towel lined bowl

2. Mix all dry ingredients in a bowl

3. In a medium fry pan add avocado oil and turn to medium heat until temperature reaches about 350-375 F

4. Scramble egg in a separate bowl

5. Lightly coat shrimp in egg then immediately place into dry mixture and roll it around to get it fully coated and drop in pan gently

6. Place shrimp in oil and cook for approx. 30 seconds per side

7. Remove shrimp and lay on a plate lined with paper towel

8. Serve with spicy mayo sauce **see pg. 82*

# PORK OMELETTE

We didn't grow up eating "breakfast food" because Laotians don't eat different foods at breakfast, lunch and dinner. However, this recipe is close since it's an omelet but it can also be enjoyed anytime of the day. This savory omelet is outstanding with the blended flavors of garlic, shallots, and green onions accompanying delicious ground pork. Think omelet meets stir-fry...heavenly.

**PREP TIME**
10 MINUTES

**COOK TIME**
20 MINUTES

**SKILL LEVEL**
EASY

**RECIPE**
KETO

**SERVINGS: 2    CALORIES: 448    FATS: 37G    PROTEIN: 20G    CARBS: 6G**

## INGREDIENTS

3 tbsps of bacon grease (from cooking bacon) or avocado oil

1 clove of minced garlic

1 medium sliced shallot

¼ sliced white onion

¼ cup of sliced green onions

⅓ lb of ground pork

1 tsp of gluten free oyster sauce

½ tbsp of fish sauce

4 medium eggs

## STEPS

1. In a medium pan, heat 3 tbsps of bacon grease (or avocado oil) for 3 minutes over medium heat

2. Add in minced garlic and sauté for 1 minute

3. After garlic is sautéed, add in pork and sauté until no longer pink

4. Add 1 tsp of oyster sauce and a pinch of salt and pepper and stir for 1 minute

5. Add shallots and onions and sauté until they become transparent

6. In a separate bowl, scramble 4 medium eggs, green onions and fish sauce and whisk all together

7. Add egg mix into the pan

8. Swirl egg mix around pan until no runny eggs

9. Flip over to cook the other side for 1 minute

10. Serve and enjoy!

# SALMON MOK

While cook-booking, this recipe was one of the most memorable ones to have our friends and family taste. It's a traditional Laotian recipe that you rarely find outside of Mom's kitchen and we have yet to find a restaurant that serves this. The salmon, spices, and herbs are enveloped and steamed together which fuses every bite into a mind-blowing delicacy. It's like Christmas for your taste buds - truly magical! This unique salmon recipe is unlike anything you've ever tasted. Bookmark this now!

**PREP TIME**
10 MINUTES +
30 MINUTES
MARINATING

**COOK TIME**
20 MINUTES

**SKILL LEVEL**
INTERMEDIATE

**RECIPE**
LOW-CARB

**SERVINGS: 4   CALORIES: 490   FATS: 27G   PROTEIN: 41G   CARBS: 15G**

## INGREDIENTS

1.5 lbs. salmon with skin on or off

1 egg

1 stalk lemongrass (5-6 inches)

1 2-inch galangal

5 kaffir lime leaves

3-10 Thai chiles

3 garlic cloves

1 large shallot

1 tbsp fish sauce

2 tbsp fermented fish (badek)

¼ tsp salt

1 cup green onions

1 cup dill

8 whole Thai chilies for garnish

## STEPS

1. Cut salmon into 1 ½ X 1 ½ inch pieces (square cubes) and add to bowl

2. Slice lemongrass, shallot, and galangal into ¼ inch pieces and add to mortar and pestle or food processor.

3. Add Thai chili, kaffir lime leaves (removing the spine of the leaves), and garlic. Pulse till incorporated, but not a paste.

4. Add mixture to salmon along with fish sauce, salt, and egg

5. Slice green onions and dill into 2 inch lengths and add to bowl and mix all ingredients well

6. Marinate in fridge for 30 minutes

7. Prepare foil for salmon. Tear approximately 11 inches of foil and place a few pieces of salmon mixture in the middle of foil. Grab opposite corners of foil and pull them together above fish. Repeat with other two corners and then fold all four corners. Repeat for other packets

8. Steam 4 packets for 20 minutes in steamer after water reaches boiling point

# BASIL SEAFOOD MEDLEY

Seafood is extremely popular in traditional Asian cuisine and you rarely find traditional cooking without seafood as an option. As kids, we grew up eating all kinds of seafood stir-fries and this classic basil medley is one that won't steer you wrong.

**PREP TIME**
10 MINUTES

**COOK TIME**
10 MINUTES

**SKILL LEVEL**
EASY

**RECIPE**
LOW-CARB

**SERVINGS: 3    CALORIES: 345    FATS: 17G    PROTEIN: 30G    CARBS: 15G**

## INGREDIENTS

6 garlic gloves

2 tbsp avocado oil

¼ white onion

8 oz. mussels

6 oz. squid

¼ cup sliced onions

1 sliced jalapeños

1 tbsp of gluten free oyster sauce

1 ½ tsp fish sauce

½ cup Thai basil

## STEPS

1. In a large nonstick pan add avocado oil over medium heat and wait for 3-5 minutes until oil is hot

2. Add garlic and sauté for 1 minute

3. Add in slices of onion and cook till semi-transparent, turn heat to low

4. Add in sliced jalapeños and sauté for 1 minute

5. Add in mussels & squid and sauté for 3 minute

6. Adjust to taste with salt and serve

# BACON CAULIFLOWER FRIED RICE

If you know nothing else about Asian cuisine, you know fried rice and every Asian subculture has their own take on it. The incredible diversity of this dish ensures that you can't get tired of it. This version is very simple to make and is sure to satisfy your fried rice craving. We like to add sriracha sauce or a little of our homemade chili oil to this dish or it can be enjoyed as is.

**PREP TIME**
10 MINUTES

**COOK TIME**
10 MINUTES

**SKILL LEVEL**
EASY

**RECIPE**
KETO

**SERVINGS: 3    CALORIES: 192    FATS: 15G    PROTEIN: 9G    CARBS: 4G**

## INGREDIENTS

1 tbsp avocado oil

1 tbsp of butter

2 cups riced cauliflower

3 slices of diced bacon

½ cup frozen veggies (remove corn if it contains it)

2 eggs

¾ tsp of liquid aminos

2 tsps of garlic powder

## STEPS

1. Over medium heat in a nonstick pan add in avocado oil and let heat for 1-2 minutes
2. Add cauliflower and sauté for 2-3 minutes. Then remove from heat off and set aside.
3. In a separate pan add butter
4. After heating butter for about 2 minutes, add diced bacon and cook thoroughly
5. Crack two eggs and scramble with bacon for about 30 seconds
6. Add frozen vegetables and stir
7. Once vegetables and egg mixture is fully incorporated, add mixture to the cooked riced cauliflower
8. Add in liquid aminos and garlic powder and mix
9. Taste and adjust with salt and pepper

# SALMON POKE BOWL

This is usually one of those meals that most would go to a restaurant and order. When you crave it as much as we do, you start to spend quite a bit money on it. That led us to wonder if we can make it at home and have it taste just as great as the restaurant's. The short answer is, absolutely! There are limitless combinations with this dish which is perfect for customizing to your taste buds. There really is no limit to what you can add.

**PREP TIME**
15 MINUTES

**COOK TIME**
5 MINUTES

**SKILL LEVEL**
EASY

**RECIPE**
KETO

**SERVINGS: 3    CALORIES: 448    FATS: 36G    PROTEIN: 36G    CARBS: 7G**

## INGREDIENTS

1 lb. of sushi grade salmon sliced into cubes (usually found at specialty seafood stores)

¼ white onion, sliced

3 tbsps of sliced green onions

1 avocado diced into cubes

1 tsp of sesame seeds

Ponzu Sauce:

4 tbsps of liquid aminos

1 tsp of sesame oil

2 ½ tsp of lemon juice

Toppings:

1 sliced jalapeño

1 oz. crushed macadamia nuts

## STEPS

1. Put salmon, white onions, green onion, sesame seeds and avocado in a bowl then set aside

2. In a separate bowl, add liquid aminos, sesame oil, lemon juice in a bowl and stir

3. Once sauce is mixed, add to the salmon bowl and mix

4. Divide into preferred serving size and top with jalapeño and macadamia nuts

# NAM TOK

It doesn't get any more simple or tasty than this. Keto-friendly and delicious, this juicy meat dish is traditionally enjoyed with sticky rice. We choose to substitute the sticky rice with cauliflower rice and a jeow (dipping sauce) of your choice. Any jeow in this book will be an excellent pairing

**PREP TIME**
5 MINUTES +
3-4 HOURS OF
MARINATING

**COOK TIME**
8 MINUTES

**SKILL LEVEL**
EASY

**RECIPE**
KETO

**SERVINGS: 2   CALORIES: 683   FATS: 57G   PROTEIN: 40G   CARBS: 0.2G**

## INGREDIENTS

1 lb. of ribeye steak

1 tbsp olive oil

¼ tsp salt

⅛ tsp pepper

½ tsp of Bragg's liquid aminos

## STEPS

1. In a gallon bag add in ribeye steak, olive oil, salt, pepper and liquid aminos. Let marinate for at least 3-4 hours

2. Heat cast iron skillet on high

3. Drizzle olive oil on cast iron skillet

4. Once the oil is hot, sear ribeye steak for 2 minutes on all sides

5. Remove from cast iron and let the ribeye steak rest for 10 minutes for the steak to reabsorb the juices

6. Slice steak into strips and enjoy!

# SPICY BAKED MUSSELS

I admit it. I'm addicted to these. Every time we go to a sushi restaurant, you can bet I'm looking to see if they have spicy baked mussels on their menu. It is an absolute favorite and we can never get enough. We knew we needed to include our personal recipe for this dish in our cookbook. The warm, creamy, savory, and mildly spicy sauce over the green mussels is to die for especially topped off with fresh green onions - yes! The best part about this is the incredible simplicity that will leave you wanting more and more. Take this a fair warning.

**PREP TIME**
10 MINUTES

**COOK TIME**
16 MINUTES

**SKILL LEVEL**
EASY

**RECIPE**
LOW-CARB

**SERVINGS: 3    CALORIES: 410    FATS: 35G    PROTEIN: 10G    CARBS: 3G**

## INGREDIENTS

12 green mussels

1 cup of olive oil mayo

2 tbsps Sriracha

¾ tsp sesame oil

1 stalk sliced green onion

## STEPS

1. Preheat oven to 350 degrees
2. In a large bowl, whisk together mayo, sriracha, sesame oil
3. Rinse off green muscles
4. Line large baking sheet with foil
5. Place green mussels on a baking sheet
6. Use a small spoon and put about 1 tbsp of spicy mayo on top of green mussels
7. Bake mussels for 15 minutes on the middle rack
8. Switch to a quick broil on high for 1 minute
9. Serve and garnish with sliced green onions

# BBQ PORK BELLY

Pork belly is one our favorite meats to eat, especially on a Keto/Low-Carb lifestyle. The taste of the BBQ mixed with the garlic, white pepper and salt along with the crispy texture and the burst of flavors from the fat makes this recipe one you'll want to revisit more than once. You won't believe how easy this is to make so don't pass this one up!

**PREP TIME**
10 MINUTES+
2 HOURS
MARINATING

**COOK TIME**
30 MINUTES

**SKILL LEVEL**
EASY

**RECIPE**
KETO

**SERVINGS: 8    CALORIES: 590    FATS: 60G    PROTEIN: 12G    CARBS: 2G**

## INGREDIENTS

2 lbs. of sliced pork belly

2 tbsp of garlic powder

2 tbsp liquid aminos

½ tsp of white pepper

¼ tsp of salt

¼ tsp of black pepper

## STEPS

1. Place pork belly in a Ziploc bag

2. Mix garlic powder, liquid aminos, white pepper, salt, and black pepper in a bowl

3. Pour mixture in the Ziploc bag

4. Massage the mixture into the pork and marinate for 2 hours

5. Bbq pork on grill for approx. 3-4 minutes per sides

6. Serve and garnish with sliced green onions.

# PAD KA PROW + FRIED EGG

Another outstanding stir-fry, this classic version boasts savory ground pork supported with the aromas of garlic, onion, basil and fresh cut Thai chilies...oh my, so tasty! The addition of a fried egg on top pushes me over the edge when I make this dish. Savory and incredibly satisfying, this simple variation hits all pleasure buttons and is a joy to eat.

**PREP TIME**
15 MINUTES

**COOK TIME**
15 MINUTES

**SKILL LEVEL**
EASY

**RECIPE**
KETO

**SERVINGS: 3    CALORIES: 534    FATS: 43G    PROTEIN: 28G    CARBS: 7G**

## INGREDIENTS

2 tbsps avocado oil

6 cloves of garlic

1 lb. of ground pork

3 oz. of long beans sliced into 2 inch pieces

½ cup of basil leaves

¼ white onion sliced

3 tsps oyster sauce

1 ½ tsp fish sauce

½ tsp liquid aminos

Pinch of salt

1 fried egg

Optional:

6 Thai chilies

## STEPS

1. Combine garlic and Thai chilies with food processor or mortar and pestle

2. Add 2 tbsp of avocado oil to a medium pan on medium heat

3. Add garlic and Thai chilies to hot oil and sauté for 1 minute

4. Add pork and a pinch of salt and sauté until the pork is no longer pink

5. Mix in oyster sauce, fish sauce, and liquid aminos

6. Sauté for 1 minute then add in onions and long beans and sauté for an additional 2 minutes

7. Remove from heat - add basil and mix

8. Taste and adjust to personal preference with salt and serve

# HAND ROLL SALMON + TUNA

Sushi lovers unite! This hand roll is a classic cone of crispy seaweed stuffed with delicious fillings to satisfy all those sushi cravings during a keto/low-carb lifestyle. By now, you know we love spice so we add heat and a little extra flavor with our spicy mayo and sriracha.

**PREP TIME**
5 MINUTES

**COOK TIME**
10 MINUTES

**SKILL LEVEL**
INTERMEDIATE

**RECIPE**
LOW-CARB

**SERVINGS: 2     CALORIES: 284     FATS: 14G     PROTEIN: 30G     CARBS: 5G**

## INGREDIENTS

4 seaweed sheets cut in half

3 oz. salmon sliced into ½ inch cubes

3 oz. tuna sliced into ½ inch cubes

½ avocado sliced into ½ inch cubes

1 carrot cut to matchstick sized pieces

Half a cucumber cut to matchstick sized pieces

## STEPS

1. Place a seaweed sheet on a cutting board add salmon, tuna, avocado, carrot, and cucumber to corner of seaweed sheet

2. Roll seaweed sheet ** should be shape of a cone**

3. Serve with ponzu sauce (pg. 26) or spicy mayo (pg. 82)

# SOUPS

# LAO BOAT

Growing up Laotian, this was an absolute household favorite! Our own version of pho (Vietnamese noodle soup), the rich and savory bone-broth is divine. Not only is this soup mouthwatering, it also helps reduce the dreaded keto-flu symptoms that are common when just starting this lifestyle. Traditionally, this is served with rice noodles which we now omit to keep our insulin levels lower and now our family doesn't even miss the noodles at all. Do yourself a favor and set aside some time to make this, you will not be disappointed!

**PREP TIME**
30 MINUTES

**COOK TIME**
1 HOUR
30 MINUTES

**SKILL LEVEL**
INTERMEDIATE

**RECIPE**
LOW-CARB

**SERVINGS: 6**    **CALORIES: 557**    **FATS: 29G**    **PROTEIN: 53G**    **CARBS: 14G**

## INGREDIENTS

---

1.5 lbs. of beef soup bones

1-1.5 lbs. of beef shank

2 packages beef meatballs

2 long stalks ginger

12 garlic cloves

1 large onion

4 celery stalks

3 whole carrots

1 bunch of cilantro steams (cut off the leaves and save leaves for garnish)

4 green onion stems (cut off the green stalk for garnish)

3 jalapeños for garnish

Basil leaves to garnish

½ thinly sliced white onion for garnish

2 Tbsps oyster sauce

2 Tbsps fish sauce

2 Tbsps chicken bouillon

2 Tbsps of beef pho flavor paste (you can find this at any Asian market)

1 1/2 Tbsps kosher salt

## STEPS

---

1. Add beef soup bones and beef shank into the soup pot then add water to the pot until water is about an inch above the meat and bones

2. Turn heat on high until water comes to a boil

3. Boil for 10 minutes or until the beef residue (fats, oils, etc.) melts off and floats to the top. Move to step #4 while you wait for the water to boil.

4. Turn oven on high broil. Broil garlic (best technique is to spear the garlic on a metal kabob skewer, it will make it easier to flip), ginger (sliced into half - long way), onion (cut into halves). You can also char the garlic, ginger and onion on a gas stove if you have one.

5. Char both sides of garlic, ginger, and onion turning over when one side is browned. **Garlic will char first so keep an close eye on it**

6. After 10 minutes of boiling, drain the pot with the bones and rinse all the residue from the bones and shank. Once clean, add meat and bones back to the pot and add fresh water. Fill up pot with water and leave about two inches from the top of the pot. Add in charred garlic, onion, ginger.

7. Cut celery stalks and carrot in half, add to pot.

8. Cut off cilantro stems from one bunch and add stems to pot. *A standard bunch is what you buy at store*

9. Cut off green onion leaves from one bunch leaving only the roots/bulb. Add roots/bulbs to pot. (Keep green stalk for garnish)

10. Add salt, oyster sauce, beef pho flavor, chicken bouillon, fish sauce to pot

11. Let soup boil on medium heat for 1 hour and 30 minutes

12. Add additional water if needed to bring soup level back to within 2 inches from the top.

13. Add 2 packets of beef meatballs

14. Turn down to simmer and serve

15. Cut garnishes (cilantro, jalapeños, green onions green stalk), pick basil leaves off stems. Garnish soup with cilantro, green onions, jalapeños, basil, bean sprouts, (optional: chili oil and sriracha).

# MIXED VEGGIE RED CURRY

A staple in our kitchen and most Thai restaurants. It was always a big deal when my mom would make it for us. As it gets colder, we eat more hearty dishes and this is one that will fill you with warm, delicious comfort no matter the temperature. The reason this dish is so common on Thai menus is the aromatic spices that electrify your taste buds coupled with the low difficultly level of preparing this dish.

**PREP TIME**
15 MINUTES

**COOK TIME**
15 MINUTES

**SKILL LEVEL**
EASY

**RECIPE**
KETO

**SERVINGS: 4    CALORIES: 460    FATS: 37G    PROTEIN: 23G    CARBS: 8G**

## INGREDIENTS

1 tbsp coconut oil

3 tbsp curry paste

1 lb. pork shoulder cut into ½ inch pieces

3 oz. yellow bell peppers, 1" squares

3 oz. red bell peppers, 1" squares

1 cup of sliced long beans or green beans

6 oz. purple eggplant, 1" cubed

1 ½ tbsp of fish sauce

1 cup of coconut milk (for step 4) + another ½ cup for step 9

½ small white onion

1 cup Thai basil leaves

Optional: Add 3-6 Thai chilies or 1 sliced jalapeño for heat

## STEPS

1. Add coconut oil to a nonstick pot over medium heat

2. Heat coconut oil for 30 seconds

3. Add curry paste to pan and sauté for 1 minute

4. Add 1 cup coconut milk and mix ingredients in pan

5. Add pork and sauté for 5 minutes

6. Add in 1 cup of chicken stock

7. When curry comes to a boil, add in Thai chilies and fish sauce

8. After a minute, add in white onions, bell peppers, long beans, eggplant, jalapeño (optional)

9. Add in remaining ½ cup of coconut milk

10. Let it simmer for 4 minutes and remove from heat

11. Add basil and stir into curry

# LAO EGG SOUP

Our father rarely cooked but when he did, this was his go-to. It truly is an original family recipe not found anywhere outside traditional Laotian homes. We are ecstatic to finally share it with the world as we know this will be a fan favorite! The fluffiness of the eggs combined with the sweetness of the shallots and onions as well as a hint of spice from the Thai chilies is a winning combination you'll swoon for.

| **PREP TIME** | **COOK TIME** | **SKILL LEVEL** | **RECIPE** |
|---|---|---|---|
| 10 MINUTES | 5 MINUTES | EASY | KETO |

**SERVINGS: 2    CALORIES: 139    FATS: 7.5G    PROTEIN: 10.6G    CARBS: 5.2G**

## INGREDIENTS

3 eggs

1 tbsp. fish sauce + (optional) 1 tsp to taste

2 cups water

1/3 cups green onions

1/3 cups shallots

2 cloves garlic

Optional:

3 Thai chilies

## STEPS

1. Thinly slice garlic, shallots, white onion, green onions, Thai chilies (optional)

2. Beat eggs into a bowl along with garlic, shallots, white onions, green onions, Thai chilies (optional) and fish sauce

3. Add water to pot and bring to a boil

4. Once water is boiling, add in egg mixture

5. Let egg mixture boil for 3 minutes

6. Give soup one light stir to barely break up egg, then serve

# TOM KHA

This soup is nothing short of flavor at its finest. Inspired by the best Tom Kha we've ever had which we stumbled upon in a Barcelona restaurant aptly called, Thai Barcelona. Who would have thought that we would have our minds blown by Thai food in Spain?! The sweet coconut-lime broth paired with tangy and tartness from the unique kaffir lime leaves and herbs will deliver bursts of flavor in every spoonful.

**PREP TIME**
15 MINUTES

**COOK TIME**
15 MINUTES

**SKILL LEVEL**
EASY

**RECIPE**
KETO

**SERVINGS: 4    CALORIES: 365    FATS: 27G    PROTEIN: 23G    CARBS: 10G**

## INGREDIENTS

6 cups chicken broth

1-inch ginger

3-inches of galangal

2 lemongrass stalks cut in 4 inches

10 kaffir lime leaves

1 ½ lbs. chicken thighs cut to 1/4 inch thickness

6 oz. mushrooms

2 tbsps and 1 tsp fish sauce

1 can coconut milk

¼ cup lime juice

Cilantro to garnish


Optional:

Chili oil

## STEPS

1. Add chicken broth, ginger, galangal, lemongrass, and kaffir lime leaves to a soup pot on high heat and bring to boil

2. Add in sliced chicken thighs

3. Let broth boil for 7 minutes

4. Add in mushrooms

5. Add in coconut milk and fish sauce and let soup boil for 2 minutes

6. Remove from heat

7. Add in lime juice

8. Garnish with cilantro and chili oil

# O M   G A I

One of our favorite food trucks of all time is this little northern Thai place in Austin, Texas called Dee-Dee. Everything on their menu is phenomenal but the Om Gai stands apart because of its uniqueness. A Thai chicken stew that dazzles the palate and boasts ample amounts of dill and other aromatic herbs floods your nose for a multi-sensory overload. After the first couple of sips, the Thai chilies start to kick in resulting in pure euphoria.

**PREP TIME**
15 MINUTES

**COOK TIME**
25 MINUTES

**SKILL LEVEL**
INTERMEDIATE

**RECIPE**
LOW-CARB

**SERVINGS: 4   CALORIES: 205   FATS: 9G   PROTEIN: 23G   CARBS: 9G**

## INGREDIENTS

2 cups of chicken broth

2 cups of water

3-8 red Thai chilies

5 cloves of garlic

1 whole lemongrass (bottom portion) or 0.7 oz.

5 pieces of galangal (¼ inch slices) or 1.3 oz.

3 kaffir lime leaves (remove from spine - just the leaf itself)

1 whole zucchini or 8 oz.

1 medium shallot

¼ white onion

1-2 oz. dill

2 oz. long beans

1 oz. basil

2 tbsps of fish sauce

2 + ½ tsp (badek) (ground preserve fish)

1 lb. of sliced chicken thigh

Salt to taste

## STEPS

1. Put chicken broth and water into pot and bring to a boil

2. In a food processor or pestle and motor put Thai chilies, lemongrass, galangal, garlic, kaffir lime leaves and pulse or mash it together. You do not want to finely grind it. You want bigger pieces (for the kaffir lime leaves, remove the spines)

3. Add herbal mixture to boiling pot and boil for 5 minutes

4. Add in sliced chicken thigh and boil for 10 minutes

5. After 10 minutes of boiling, add in fish sauce, badek, long beans, zucchini, white onion and let soup boil for 5 minutes until vegetables are cooked

6. Stir in dill and basil and boil for 1 minute

7. Remove from heat and serve

# KIMCHI JJIGAE

One of our favorite things to do in Los Angeles is go to Koreatown and enjoy some delicious Korean BBQ. Kimchi (fermented Napa cabbage) is a staple that will accompany a variety of dishes and our love for Korean flavors inspired us to have this traditional recipe. This dish is sour, tangy, savory, and salty all in one satisfying slurp.

**PREP TIME**
5 MINUTES

**COOK TIME**
15 MINUTES

**SKILL LEVEL**
EASY

**RECIPE**
KETO

**SERVINGS: 4    CALORIES: 526    FATS: 50G    PROTEIN: 10G    CARBS: 4G**

## INGREDIENTS

10 oz. sliced pork belly cut into 1 inch squares

1 cup kimchi

2 cup chicken stock

¼ tsp salt

¼ tsp pepper

1 stalk green onions cut diagonally

Serranoes or jalapeños cut diagonally

## STEPS

1. In a nonstick soup pot, sear sliced pork belly over high heat until browned/cooked

2. Reduce heat to medium, add kimchi, and stir for 1 minute

3. Add in chicken stock, salt and pepper and boil for 5 minutes then remove from heat

4. Cut green onions, serranoes or jalapenos (optional) and garnish soup

# SALADS

# CUCUMBER SALAD

Similar to the papaya salad, the cucumber salad is a light and flavorful compliment to so many Asian dishes. In the west, cucumber is easier to find than papaya and is typically more familiar to most people as well. I like to think of it as a beginner's papaya salad! Pair this with a meat dish to balance the incredible spectrum of flavors.

**PREP TIME**
15 MINUTES

**COOK TIME**
10 MINUTES

**SKILL LEVEL**
INTERMEDIATE

**RECIPE**
LOW-CARB

**SERVINGS: 3     CALORIES: 36     FATS: 1G     PROTEIN: 1G     CARBS: 6G**

## INGREDIENTS

8 oz. shredded cucumber

½ tsp of fermented shrimp paste

10 cherry tomatoes

½ lime

1 tbsp of fish sauce

2 tsp of badek

## STEPS

1. Using a mortar and pestle, combine Thai chilies, shrimp paste and a pinch of salt. Pound ingredients together until it becomes a paste. *If you do not have a mortar or pestle, use a food processor and pulse until combined (do not finely grind)*

2. Add cherry tomatoes and mash with pestle while stirring with a spoon, alternating the pestle and spoon

3. Add fish sauce, badek and squeeze lime in mixture and stir

4. Add shredded cucumber to mortar. Alternate *gently* mashing with the pestle and stirring with the spoon to combine the mixture. *If you are using a food processor, put shredded cucumber in a bowl and pour sauce over the bowl and combine it all together. Don't put the cucumber in the processor*

5. Taste and adjust with lime and fish sauce to your liking then serve

# CHOPPED CHICKEN ASIAN SALAD + SESAME VINAIGRETTE

What's more refreshing on a hot summer day than a crisp, fresh salad? This classic dish perfectly marries crunchy veggies and a sublime sesame vinaigrette dressing tossed together for a perfect combination.

**PREP TIME**
10 MINUTES

**COOK TIME**
20 MINUTES

**SKILL LEVEL**
EASY

**RECIPE**
KETO

**SERVINGS: 2   CALORIES: 378   FATS: 28G   PROTEIN: 26G   CARBS: 4G**

## INGREDIENTS

Salad:

3 skinless chicken thigh filets or

8 oz.

1 tsp avocado oil

⅛ tsp salt

¼ tsp pepper

8 oz. chopped romaine

⅓ cup julienned green onions

2 oz. julienned red cabbage

½ of large avocado

2 oz. julienned carrots

Sesame seeds as a garnish

Slivered almonds as a garnish

Dressing:

½ tsp sesame seed oil

2 tbsps apple cider vinegar

¾ tsp liquid aminos

⅛ tsp black pepper

⅛ tsp salt to taste

## STEPS

1. Season chicken thighs with salt and pepper

2. Grill chicken thighs over direct medium heat for about 10 minutes. Turn and cook until almost done, another 5-10 minutes, depending on size chicken thigh and set aside chicken when it's done

3. In a bowl, whisk sesame seed oil, apple cider vinegar, liquid aminos, black pepper and salt

4. In a different bowl, add Romaine, chicken, cabbage, carrots, green onions. Add dressing and toss.

# YUM SALAD

A household favorite! This salad is one you will find only in home cooking and at Laotian gatherings and events. The creamy egg dressing paired with the savory sautéed pork over a bed of crispy-refreshing romaine, herbs and tomato mixture is to die for! You must try this unique salad recipe!

**PREP TIME**
25 MINUTES

**COOK TIME**
20 MINUTES

**SKILL LEVEL**
INTERMEDIATE

**RECIPE**
KETO

**SERVINGS: 3**   **CALORIES: 593**   **FATS: 47G**   **PROTEIN: 26G**   **CARBS: 9G**

## INGREDIENTS

2 tbsps of avocado oil

3 garlic cloves

½ lb. thinly sliced pork

1 tbsp of gluten-free oyster sauce

1 tsp of fish sauce

5 cups of sliced Romaine lettuce

1 cup sliced tomato or 1 medium tomato

1 cup of sliced cucumber or 8 oz.

½ of cup cilantro (cut into 1 ½ inch pieces)

½ of cup julienned green onions (sliced vertically about 2 inches long)

¼ cup shelled peanuts

4 hard boiled eggs (cut in half and separate egg yolks from egg whites)

Dressing:

⅓ cup of mayonnaise

4 boils egg yolks

2 tsp of fish sauce

1 ½ tsp of lime juice

## STEPS

Pork:

1. Add in 2 tbsps of avocado oil to a nonstick pan over medium heat for 30 seconds. Add garlic and sauté for 30 seconds. Then add pork and sauté pork for one minute

2. Add oyster sauce and fish sauce to pan and sauté for 8 minutes until fully cooked and browned. Once done, set pork aside to cool down

Peanuts:

3. On a separate nonstick pan over medium heat add in skinless peanuts to roast. Constantly stir until peanuts turn medium brown. Set aside peanuts to cool down to room temperature

4. Add roasted peanuts to mortar and use pestle to mash peanuts or put roasted peanuts in a sandwich bag and mash with a rolling pin. *Do not finely grind*

Boil Egg:

5. Boil eggs for 12 minutes until hard boiled

6. Remove eggs from boiling water and place in a bowl of ice water

7. After 5 minutes, peel and slice eggs in half. Remove egg yolks (set aside for dressing)

8. Slice egg whites halves into 3-4 slices

Dressing:

9. Add mayo, egg yolks, fish sauce and lime juice into a food processor. Pulse dressing until smooth consistency

Salad:

10. In a big bowl combine Romaine lettuce, tomatoes, cucumbers, green onions, cilantro, egg whites, peanuts, pork and mix all together with dressing

# PAPAYA SALAD

When we think of Laotian cuisine - this is the first dish that comes to mind. We call it "Thum" which means to mash in our traditional pestle and mortar. Every bite of this versatile dish strives to achieve a complete taste profile yielding sweet, sour, salty, spicy and savory. However, it is totally customizable to your own preference. We love it without the sweetness (i.e. sugar) as we strive for a healthier yet still amazingly tasty option. Here we show you how to make it with the coveted raw-green papaya and cucumber. We suggest that you pair this with a meat dish, preferably something BBQ. We highly recommend the BBQ Moo Ping recipe (see pg. 12). This combination is a sure winner and is one of our favorite meals we make!

| PREP TIME | COOK TIME | SKILL LEVEL | RECIPE |
|---|---|---|---|
| 15 MINUTES | 10 MINUTES | INTERMEDIATE | LOW-CARB |

**SERVINGS: 3     CALORIES: 51     FATS: 1G     PROTEIN: 2G     CARBS: 9G**

## INGREDIENTS

3-6 Thai chilies (mild) 6-9 (hot-hot)

8 oz. shredded green papaya

½ tsp of fermented shrimp paste

10 cherry tomatoes, halved

½ small lime

1 tbsp of fish sauce

2 tsp badek

(Optional version #2)

½ tsp of fermented crab paste

½ tsp of fermented shrimp paste

1 tbsp of fish sauce

1 tbsp badek

## STEPS

1. Using a mortar and pestle combine Thai chilies, shrimp paste and a pinch of salt (if making version 2, add crab paste as well). Pound ingredients together until it becomes a paste. *If you do not have a mortar or pestle, use a food processor and pulse until combined (do not finely grind)*

2. Add cherry tomatoes and mash with pestle while alternating tossing the mixture with a spoon

3. (Optional version #2) Add fish sauce, badek and squeeze lime in mixture and stir

4. Add shredded papaya to mortar. Alternate gently mashing with the pestle and stirring with the spoon to combine the mixture
   *If you are using a food processor, put shredded papaya in a bowl and pour sauce over the bowl and combine it all together*

5. Adjust to taste with lime and fish sauce

# CUCUMBER KIMCHI

Whenever we go to Korean BBQ restaurants, we hope they have cucumber kimchi as a side dish. Every restaurant is a little different so the side dishes change frequently and it's not always guaranteed they have it available. Since we can't rely on the restaurants to satisfy our cravings, we developed our own. One of the easiest and tastiest recipes in this cookbook, we recommend that you try this with our BBQ Pork Belly recipe as the Koreans are known for their delightful BBQ and kimchi pairing!

**PREP TIME**
5 MINUTES

**COOK TIME**
5 MINUTES

**SKILL LEVEL**
EASY

**RECIPE**
LOW-CARB

**SERVINGS: 2     CALORIES: 72     FATS: 5G     PROTEIN: 4G     CARBS: 9G**

## INGREDIENTS

1 medium English cucumber or 13 oz. (sliced)

¼ thinly sliced white onion or ¼ cup

1 stalk green onions

2 garlic cloves minced

2 tbsps liquid aminos

2 tsps Korean hot pepper flakes

2 tsps sesame oil

2 tsps sesame seeds

¼ tsp of lemon juice

## STEPS

1. Combine all ingredients and serve

# SIDES

# TEPPANYAKI ZOODLES

One of our favorite memories in college was meeting up for lunch at a local Japanese restaurant eating teppanyaki. Along with the great food, we got an awesome show from the chefs. We were instant fans of what was served especially the mixed veggies (zucchini, onions, mushrooms and sprouts). Inspired by our teppanyaki days, we knew we had to include this recipe for our cookbook. The crunchy, buttery, and savory profile of this recipe will quench your noodle cravings and makes for the perfect side dish for all meats, especially a grilled steak!

**PREP TIME**
15 MINUTES

**COOK TIME**
10 MINUTES

**SKILL LEVEL**
EASY

**RECIPE**
KETO

**SERVINGS: 2    CALORIES: 287    FATS: 29G    PROTEIN: 7G    CARBS: 9G**

## INGREDIENTS

2 medium shredded zucchini (do not shred core/seeds, only the firm outer part)

1 cup of bean sprouts

½ sliced white onion

4 oz. sliced mushrooms

2 tbsps of Bragg's liquid aminos

¼ tsp of white vinegar

2 tsp of sesame seed

4 tbsps of butter

## STEPS

1. On a nonstick pan over medium heat, add in butter
2. Once the butter has melted, add in white onions and mushrooms and sauté
3. Once the onions are transparent add in shredded zucchini noodles
4. Sauté until the zucchini has softened then add in bean sprouts
5. Add liquid aminos and white vinegar
6. Sauté all vegetables together for 3-5 minutes
7. Sprinkle sesame seed on top, mix together

# GARLIC CHINESE BROCCOLI

Chinese Broccoli is extremely common in Asian cuisine for its ability to pair so well with a wide range of dishes. If you're not familiar, it is sort of like a cross between collard greens and regular broccoli. Simple to make, the slightly bitter taste of the broccoli married with the fresh aroma of garlic which is balanced by the liquid aminos is all this dish needs for all us veggie lovers. Substitute broccolini if you cannot find Chinese broccoli.

**PREP TIME**
5 MINUTES

**COOK TIME**
5 MINUTES

**SKILL LEVEL**
EASY

**RECIPE**
KETO

**SERVINGS: 2     CALORIES: 210     FATS: 21G     PROTEIN: 1G     CARBS: 4G**

## INGREDIENTS

10 oz. Chinese broccoli (sliced into 4 inch sections)

3 tbsps of avocado oil

6 garlic cloves (sliced)

½ tbsp liquid aminos

## STEPS

1. In a nonstick pan and medium heat, add avocado oil
2. After 2 minutes add in sliced garlic
3. Sauté garlic for 1 minute
4. Add in Chinese broccoli and saute for 3-5 minutes to desired texture
5. Add in liquid aminos
6. Salt and pepper to taste

# ONG CHOY STIR-FRY
# (ASIAN WATER SPINACH)

Traditional Asian households eat a wide assortment of vegetables. We didn't have the luxury growing up to be picky eaters because what was served to you, you would eat or you would go to bed hungry! Luckily for us, we loved 90% of the vegetables served to us and this Chinese water spinach is one of them. The mild taste with a slightly nutty undertone is complimented so well with the accent of garlic and Thai chilies. This side dish was always cooked with your protein of choice.

**PREP TIME**
5 MINUTES

**COOK TIME**
5 MINUTES

**SKILL LEVEL**
EASY

**RECIPE**
KETO

**SERVINGS: 2    CALORIES: 215    FATS: 21G    PROTEIN: 1G    CARBS: 5G**

## INGREDIENTS

6 oz. Ong-Choy (water spinach)

5 small minced garlic gloves

3 tbsps olive oil

¾ tsp fish sauce

1 tbsp oyster sauce

3 Thai chilies

## STEPS

1. Over medium heat in a nonstick sauce pan add olive oil

2. Add in garlic and Thai chilies and sauté till garlic becomes golden brown

3. Add water spinach and sauté for 2 minutes (water spinach will wilt down)

4. Mix in oyster sauce and fish sauce

5. Taste and adjust with salt and pepper

# BLISTERED SHISHITO PEPPERS

We had these for the first time as an appetizer at a sushi restaurant and couldn't get them out of our minds (and hearts) ever since. Although these Japanese peppers may look intimidating at first glance, they're surprisingly mild with outstanding flavor. Blistering these peppers gives it a smoky taste that is just right. We sprinkle it with our favorite mild salt, fleur de sel, and pair it with a spicy mayo aioli that is to die for! The perfect side dish/appetizer which everyone will love.

**PREP TIME**
5 MINUTES

**COOK TIME**
10 MINUTES

**SKILL LEVEL**
EASY

**RECIPE**
KETO

**SERVINGS: 2    CALORIES: 380    FATS: 38G    PROTEIN: 1G    CARBS: 2G**

## INGREDIENTS

2 tbsps avocado oil

6 oz. shishito peppers

Pinch of fleur de sel


Sauce:

½ cup of mayo

1 tsp of Sriracha

¼ tsp of sesame oil

## STEPS

1. Whisk mayo, Sriracha, and sesame oil in a bowl and set aside

2. Add 2 tbsps of avocado oil to nonstick pan over medium-high heat, let the oil heat up until hot (3 minutes)

3. Add shishito peppers to pan and toss until peppers are blistered and charred (3-5 minutes)

4. Dip shishito peppers in spicy mayo and enjoy!

# SAUTÉED BOK CHOY

Bok Choy is one of the best vegetables you can eat and it meshes perfectly with the Keto Diet! Healthy and extremely tasty, it can be cooked in wide variety of ways but our favorite version is sautéed. The juicy stalks and green leaves absorb the garlic and liquid aminos enhancing it to full flavor with a slightly sweet undertone.

**PREP TIME**
5 MINUTES

**COOK TIME**
5 MINUTES

**SKILL LEVEL**
EASY

**RECIPE**
KETO

**SERVINGS: 2    CALORIES: 140    FATS: 14G    PROTEIN: 2G    CARBS: 4G**

## INGREDIENTS

2 tbsps of avocado oil

5 large minced garlic cloves

10 oz. bok choy sliced about a ½ inch from the root

¾ tbsp liquid aminos

## STEPS

1. In a nonstick pan over medium heat, add avocado oil for 1-2 minutes

2. Add garlic and sauté until lightly brown

3. Add bok choy and sauté until greens are wilted

4. Add liquid aminos and remove from heat

5. Taste and adjust as needed with salt and serve

# SAUTÉED LONG BEANS

The great thing about long beans is that they're so versatile. Hot or cold, cooked or raw, they taste great. Here we have the classic sautéed variation. The nutty-crunchy flavor of the long beans sautéed with the garlic and oyster sauce brings this stir-fry to a new level. This dish is so tasty that you'll enjoy it solo or paired with your protein of choice.

**PREP TIME**
5 MINUTES

**COOK TIME**
10 MINUTES

**SKILL LEVEL**
EASY

**RECIPE**
LOW-CARB

**SERVINGS: 2    CALORIES: 184    FATS: 14G    PROTEIN: 3G    CARBS: 12G**

## INGREDIENTS

2 tbsps of avocado oil

2 cups of long beans (cut into 1-2 inches)

4 cloves of minced garlic

4 tsps fish sauce

½ tbsp gluten free oyster sauce

## STEPS

1. Over medium heat in a nonstick pan, add avocado oil

2. After 3 minutes add in garlic

3. After 1 minute add in long beans, fish sauce, and oyster sauce

4. Sauté and constantly stir for 5 minutes or until desired texture is reached

5. Salt and pepper to taste

# SAUCES

# CHILI OIL

You can't go to an Asian restaurant without finding this on the table. However, freshly homemade chili oil adds another dimension of flavor that is lacking from what has probably turned rancid and been sitting on that table for a few months. We love making it ourselves because this helps us ensure the quality of the oil and the desired spiciness level. This chili oil is meant to be stored in an airtight container and as the oil infuses over time, it continues to improve its flavor! You can top on any food desired and it is sure to have a permanent home in your pantry.

**PREP TIME**
5 MINUTES

**COOK TIME**
8-10 MINUTES

**SKILL LEVEL**
EASY

**RECIPE**
KETO

**SERVINGS: 70    CALORIES: 43    FATS: 5G    PROTEIN: 0G    CARBS: 0.3G**

## INGREDIENTS

1 ½ cup avocado oil

½ cup minced of garlic

¾ cup ground up dried chili (if you would like spicier, you can up it to 1 cup)

Equipment: 500 ml (16 oz. jar)

## STEPS

1. In a nonstick pan over medium heat add in avocado oil

2. After oil starts to simmer add in garlic

3. Let garlic cook for 1 minute in oil

4. Add in dried ground up chili flakes

5. Turn heat down to low

6. Simmer and constantly stir the chili oil mixture with a spatula until chili flake skin turns burgundy or dark red to light brown (approximately 8-10 minutes)

7. If you prefer a really smoky flavor, keep stirring the chili oil until medium brown (10-12 minutes)

8. Remove from heat and let cool before storing it in a glass mason jar

# SPICY MAYO

A staple of all sushi restaurants. We always ask our server to bring extra to the table because of the elevated flavor that accompanies this delicious sauce. The toasted sesame is balanced with sriracha and a creamy texture that is so simple yet adds so much flavor to anything you drizzle this on.

**PREP TIME**
1 MINUTES

**COOK TIME**
3 MINUTES

**SKILL LEVEL**
EASY

**RECIPE**
KETO

**SERVINGS: 3    CALORIES: 164    FATS: 16G    PROTEIN: 0G    CARBS: 0G**

## INGREDIENTS

½ cup of mayonnaise

1 tsp of Sriracha

¼ tsp of sesame oil

Optional:

Sesame seeds to garnish if desired

## STEPS

1. Add mayo, sriracha, and sesame oil to small bowl

2. Mix all ingredients together until well combined

3. Add sesame seeds to garnish if desired

# MUSHROOM JEOW

For Laotians, jeow is a must-have dipping sauce for sides and entrees. Texture and consistency varies widely as it can be made from a variety of vegetables, spices, and herbs. We are big fans of mushrooms and knew we couldn't do a cookbook without including this recipe. The fresh herbs and spices transform the mushrooms into a unique medley that will shock your taste buds. There is nothing like it in any restaurant you've been to and if you're a mushroom fan, you're in for a treat!

| PREP TIME | COOK TIME | SKILL LEVEL | RECIPE |
|---|---|---|---|
| 5 MINUTES | 20 MINUTES | EASY | LOW-CARB |

**SERVINGS: 2    CALORIES: 34    FATS: 0.1G    PROTEIN: 2G    CARBS: 4G**

## INGREDIENTS

8 oz. mushrooms

2-3 garlic cloves

10 Thai chilies

1 stalk green onions

1 large shallot

1 tbsp chopped cilantro

1 tbsp fish sauce

Pinch of salt

Optional:
1 sliced English cucumber

## STEPS

1. Broil mushrooms, garlic cloves, chili peppers, green onions, and shallot on a baking pan until vegetables have a medium char. (note: chili peppers and garlic cloves will char first)

2. After vegetables are charred, add all ingredients to a food processor and pulse gently (if using mortar, add chili, green onion stem, shallot and garlic first. Then add mushrooms last)

3. After everything is mixed, add fish sauce and a pinch of salt

4. Taste and adjust as needed with salt and fish sauce

5. Add cilantro and mix well

6. Serve mushroom jeow on top of sliced cucumber and enjoy

# TOMATO JEOW

The standard jeow served in many Thai/Lao restaurants. It's easy, fresh, and goes especially well with meats. It'll make you wonder, "Where has this been all my life?!" A lot of people compare this to salsa but the flavor of it is nothing like the salsa you are used to. The roasted vegetables are mashed with the secret ingredient, fish sauce, giving it southeast Asian flair.

**PREP TIME**

5 MINUTES

**COOK TIME**

20 MINUTES

**SKILL LEVEL**

EASY

**RECIPE**

LOW-CARB

**SERVINGS: 2    CALORIES: 58    FATS: 0.2G    PROTEIN: 2G    CARBS: 10G**

## INGREDIENTS

10.5 oz. of cherry tomatoes

1 medium shallot

4 cloves of garlic

6 Thai chilies

¼ tsp of salt

1 tbsp of fish sauce

1 tbsp of cilantro

## STEPS

1.  Skewer the shallots, garlic, and Thai chilies

2.  Broil on high until skewers are charred on both sides (keep a close eye on these with the oven light on)

3.  Put cherry tomatoes on a baking sheet and broil on high - flip both sides making sure the majority of the tomato skin is charred

4.  Add Thai chilies, garlic, and shallot to food processor and blend or mash with pestle and mortar

5.  After blending, add in tomatoes and lightly pulse or mash

6.  Add fish sauce and salt.

7.  Add chopped cilantro, stir, and serve

# SPICY LEMONGRASS JEOW

T his was the seafood sauce that every kid in our family requested our mom to make all the time! The freshness of the aromatic herbs and spices combine for a favor profile that is tangy and spicy. You'll never want to eat seafood again without this jeow.

**PREP TIME**
5 MINUTES

**COOK TIME**
1 MINUTES

**SKILL LEVEL**
EASY

**RECIPE**
LOW-CARB

**SERVINGS: 2    CALORIES: 43    FATS: 0G    PROTEIN: 2G    CARBS: 8G**

## INGREDIENTS

3 tbsp fish sauce

2 tbsp lime + 1 tsp for later

⅛ tsp salt

3-4 cloves garlic

3 ½ inches or 1 stalk of lemongrass (just the base of the lemongrass, sliced thinly)

3-10 Thai chilies

1 inch or 0.5 oz. of ginger

1 tbsp cilantro (chopped, garnish)

## STEPS

1. Add Thai chilies, garlic, lemongrass, and ginger to food processor (or mortar and pestle) Blend/pound until everything is mixed together

2. Mix in fish sauce and lime juice

3. Scoop everything out to small bowl, garnish with cilantro

4. Adjust taste as needed with salt

# JEOW SOM

In Laotian, som means sour. This jeow strikes the perfect balance of fresh, sour, and tangy to achieve an oh-so-mouth-watering result! We love this sauce for all our favorite grilled meats.

**PREP TIME**
5 MINUTES

**COOK TIME**
5 MINUTES

**SKILL LEVEL**
EASY

**RECIPE**
KETO

**SERVINGS: 2    CALORIES: 23    FATS: 0G    PROTEIN: 1G    CARBS: 4G**

## INGREDIENTS

3 cloves of garlic

3-7 Thai chilies

1 tbsp lime juice

1 tbsp of fish sauce

1 ¼ tsp of salt

1 tsp of chopped cilantro

## STEPS

1. In a mortar or food processor add garlic, Thai chilies, lime, fish sauce, salt

2. Blend or mash until everything is mixed together

3. Pour in a small bowl and garnish with chopped cilantro

4. Adjust to taste with salt, if desired

Made in the USA
Middletown, DE
28 March 2020